WOODLAND WILDLIFE

Red Foxes

by G. G. Lake

CAPSTONE PRESS
a capstone imprint

Pebble®
Plus

Pebble Plus is published by Capstone Press,
1710 Roe Crest Drive, North Mankato, Minnesota 56003
www.mycapstone.com

Library of Congress Cataloging-in-Publication Data
Names: Lake, G. G., author.
Title: Red foxes / by G. G. Lake.
Description: North Mankato, Minnesota : Capstone Press, [2017] | Series:
  Pebble plus. Woodland wildlife | Audience: Ages 4–8 | Audience: K to
  grade 3 | Includes bibliographical references and index.
Identifiers: LCCN 2016002043| ISBN 9781515708155 (library binding) | ISBN
  9781515708223 (pbk.) | ISBN 9781515708285 (ebook (pdf))
Subjects: LCSH: Red fox—Juvenile literature.
Classification: LCC QL737.C22 L2547 2017 | DDC 599.775—dc23
LC record available at http://lccn.loc.gov/2016002043

Editorial Credits
Gena Chester, editor; Juliette Peters, designer;
Wanda Winch, media researcher; Steve Walker, production specialist

Photo Credits
Dreamstime: Menno67, 17; Shutterstock: alicedaniel, illustrated forest items, Anna
Subbotina, 22-23, AR Pictures,tree bark design, Bildagentur Zoonar GmbH, 13, Daniel
Hebert, 15, Darlene Hewson, 9, elina, 24, Holly Kuchera, 19, Andrew Astbury, 5, Mark
Bridger, cover, Menno Schaefer, 11 (top), 21, mythja, 1, Pim Leijen, 7, Stawek, 11 (map),
Sunny Forest, 3

Note to Parents and Teachers

The Woodland Wildlife set supports national curriculum standards for science related
to life science. This book describes and illustrates red foxes. The images support
early readers in understanding the text. The repetition of words and phrases
helps early readers learn new words. This book also introduces early readers to
subject-specific vocabulary words, which are defined in the Glossary section. Early
readers may need assistance to read some words and to use the Table of Contents,
Glossary, Read More, Internet Sites, Critical Thinking Using the Common Core,
and Index sections of the book.

Printed and bound in China
PO007726LEOF16

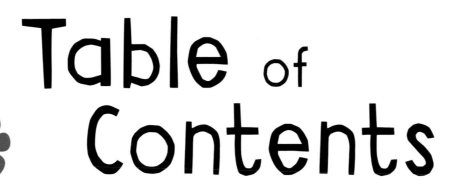

Table of Contents

Red Foxes

The stars twinkle high above the trees.

A red fox roams the forest floor.

Its pointed nose smells for food.

Most red foxes have red, black, and white fur in their coats. But a few red foxes don't have any red fur. These foxes have black, silver, or golden coats.

7

Red foxes have black fur
on their legs and on the backs
of their ears. Their bushy tails have
a white tip. White fur grows
around their noses.

Forest Homes

Foxes live in many places.
They may live in deserts or
near mountains. But they usually live
in the woods and near meadows.

Red Fox Range Map

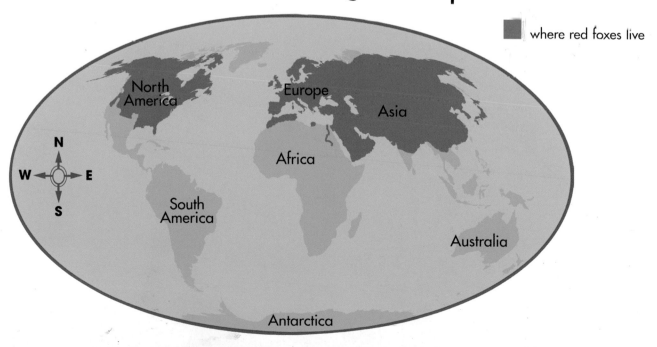

where red foxes live

North America

Europe

Asia

Africa

South America

Australia

Antarctica

N
W E
S

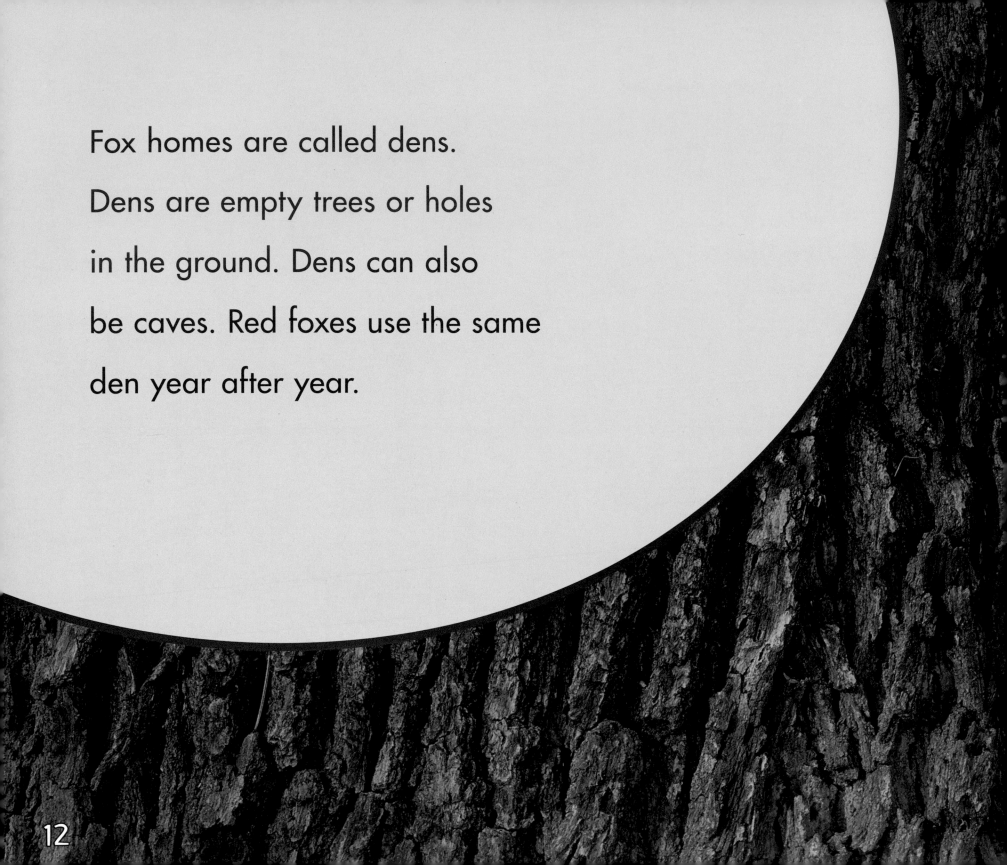

Fox homes are called dens.
Dens are empty trees or holes
in the ground. Dens can also
be caves. Red foxes use the same
den year after year.

Hunting

Red foxes hunt alone at night. They usually eat rodents and other small animals. Foxes use their noses to find rodent dens.

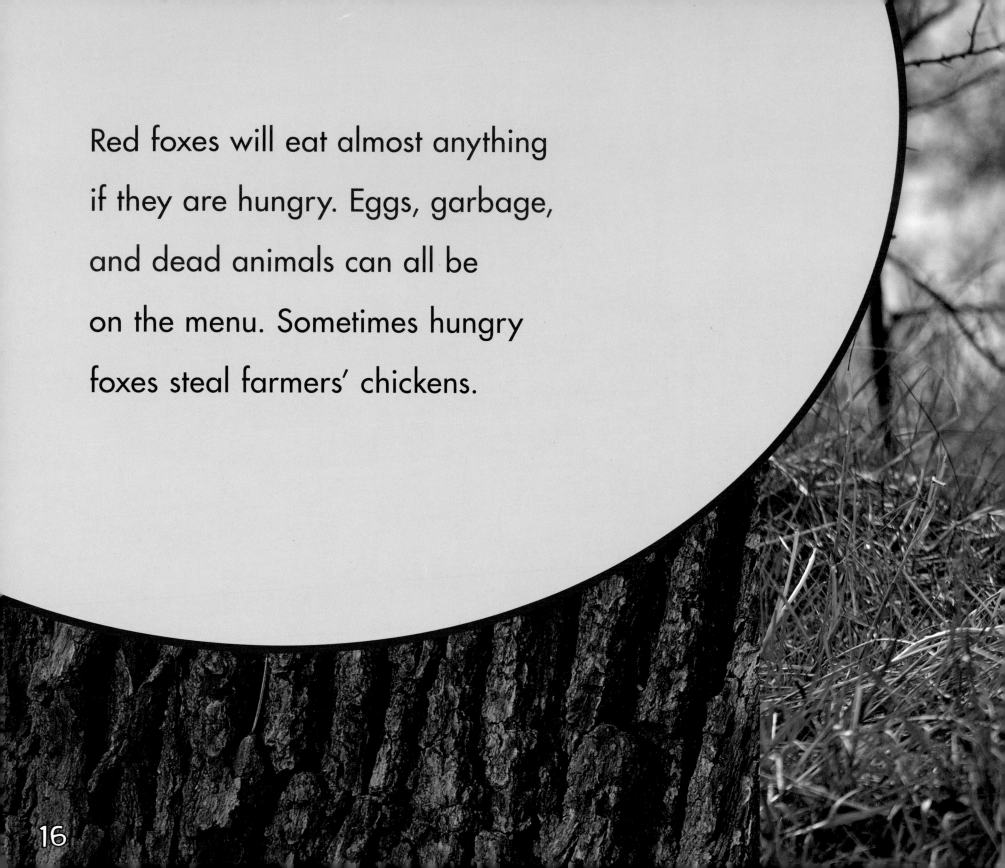

Red foxes will eat almost anything if they are hungry. Eggs, garbage, and dead animals can all be on the menu. Sometimes hungry foxes steal farmers' chickens.

Fox Pups

Mother foxes can have up to
10 babies at a time. Baby foxes
are called pups. The pups are
born gray. Their fur changes
color after a month.

Both the mother and father take
care of pups for six months.
The parents must watch
for predators. Coyotes, cougars,
and lynx hunt fox pups.

Glossary

den—a place where a wild animal may live; a den may be a hole in the ground or a trunk of a tree

fur—thick hair that covers an animal

lynx—a wildcat with long legs, a short tail, light brown or orange fur, and tufts of hair on its ears

meadow—a big, usually low area of land that is mostly covered with grass

predator—an animal that hunts other animals for food

pup—a young fox

woods—a large area covered with trees and plants; forests are sometimes called woods

Read More

Orr, Nicole. *Red Foxes.* Kennett Square, Penn.: Purple Toad Publishing, 2015.

Rissman, Rebecca. *Red Foxes: Nocturnal Predators.* North Mankato, Minn.: Capstone Press, 2015.

Strother, Ruth. *Red Foxes.* New York: Bearport Publishing, 2014.

Internet Sites

FactHound offers a safe, fun way to find Internet sites related to this book. All of the sites on FactHound have been researched by our staff.

Here's all you do:

Visit *www.facthound.com*

Type in this code: 9781515708155

Super-cool stuff!

Check out projects, games and lots more at
www.capstonekids.com

Critical Thinking
Using the Common Core

1. Why do you think farmers might not like red foxes?
   (Integration of Knowledge and Ideas)

2. What different colors of fur can a red fox have?
   (Key Ideas and Details)

3. What is a den? (Key Ideas and Details)

Index